Lisa Hammond, ...
and Lee Simpson

STILL NO IDEA

OBERON BOOKS
LONDON

WWW.OBERONBOOKS.COM

First published in 2018 by Oberon Books Ltd
521 Caledonian Road, London N7 9RH
Tel: +44 (0) 20 7607 3637 / Fax: +44 (0) 20 7607 3629
e-mail: info@oberonbooks.com
www.oberonbooks.com

PB ISBN: 9781786826947
E ISBN: 9781786826930

Cover image: Idil Sukan

Printed and bound by 4EDGE Limited, Hockley, Essex, UK.
eBook conversion by Lapiz Digital Services, India.

10 9 8 7 6 5 4 3 2 1

Lisa Hammond and Rachael Spence

Lisa and Rachael have been producing work together for the last ten years. Their friendship and their take on the world is honest, brutal and full of love. They work across television, theatre and community performance projects. Their joint credits include *Still No Idea* (with Improbable and the Royal Court Theatre); *Lowdown* (a Channel 4 comedy, Blap with Retort); *Old Street New Street* (with Shoreditch Town Hall); *Wolfgang and The Princess* (Barbican pit labs); *Helena and Hermia* (RSC studio) and *No Idea* (with Improbable at the Young Vic). They have also been commissioned by the Globe Theatre to create a piece for their *Dark Night of The Soul* event in Winter 2018 and they were selected for BAFTA Elevate 2018.

Both have very successful independent acting careers with numerous theatre, film, television and radio credits between them, including the National Theatre, Globe, National Theatre of Scotland and Wales, RSC, Royal Exchange, Brooklyn Academy of Music (BAM), Sydney Opera House, BBC Television and radio, ITV, CH4 and Sky Atlantic.

They have recently formed a brand-new artistic partnership called **Bunny** to create work that gets us talking. Bunny is short for rabbit, cockney rhyming slang for 'Talk' – 'Rabbit and Pork, Talk.'

www.bunnyproductions.co.uk

Improbable

"What kind of theatre do you make?" is a question people often ask. It's difficult to give a simple answer because Improbable goes in many directions at once. Each project has a different creative team—sometimes people we've worked with a lot, sometimes people we've never worked with before. Sometimes the work is big, like *Sticky*, an outdoor piece with giant transparent tape structures; sometimes it's in big spaces like *Theatre of Blood* at the National Theatre, or *Satyagraha and Akhnaten* at the English National Opera; and sometimes it's smaller like *Animo, Permission Improbable*, and *Lost Without Words*. Shows could be improvised, scripted, or devised; sometimes there's even acting. We've taken shows all over the world from Sydney to Syria, New York to nearly everywhere else. For the last ten years, we've hosted and facilitated Open Space Technology events under the banner of "Devoted and Disgruntled." Open Space is a self-organising process enabling large groups to tackle complex issues with no formal agenda. These events have seen the emergence of a nationwide community of artists and theatre practitioners who have created projects, partnerships, shows, companies, and venues. And we also run the International Institute of Improvisation, connecting improvisers working in the arts, sciences and business across the world.

Improbable is a charity and we have ambitious fundraising targets to meet in order to keep producing our work. We rely on the support of people who are excited by our vision and want to help shape the company's future.

To find out more about Improbable,
visit **www.improbable.co.uk**
or follow us on Twitter **@Improbable1**

Supported using public funding by
ARTS COUNCIL ENGLAND

Improbable is a National Portfolio Organisation of Arts Council England

THE ROYAL COURT THEATRE

The Royal Court Theatre is the writers' theatre. It is a leading force in world theatre for energetically cultivating writers – undiscovered, emerging and established.

Through the writers, the Royal Court is at the forefront of creating restless, alert, provocative theatre about now. We open our doors to the unheard voices and free thinkers that, through their writing, change our way of seeing.

Over 120,000 people visit the Royal Court in Sloane Square, London, each year and many thousands more see our work elsewhere through transfers to the West End and New York, UK and international tours, digital platforms, our residencies across London, and our site-specific work. Through all our work we strive to inspire audiences and influence future writers with radical thinking and provocative discussion.

The Royal Court's extensive development activity encompasses a diverse range of writers and artists and includes an ongoing programme of writers' attachments, readings, workshops and playwriting groups. Twenty years of the International Department's pioneering work around the world means the Royal Court has relationships with writers on every continent.

Within the past sixty years, John Osborne, Samuel Beckett, Arnold Wesker, Ann Jellicoe, Howard Brenton and David Hare have started their careers at the Court. Many others including Caryl Churchill, Athol Fugard, Mark Ravenhill, Simon Stephens, debbie tucker green, Sarah Kane – and, more recently, Lucy Kirkwood, Nick Payne, Penelope Skinner and Alistair McDowall – have followed.

The Royal Court has produced many iconic plays from Lucy Kirkwood's **The Children** to Jez Butterworth's **Jerusalem** and Martin McDonagh's **Hangmen**.

Royal Court plays from every decade are now performed on stage and taught in classrooms and universities across the globe.

It is because of this commitment to the writer that we believe there is no more important theatre in the world than the Royal Court.

Supported using public funding by
**ARTS COUNCIL
ENGLAND**

Production shots © Camilla Greenwell

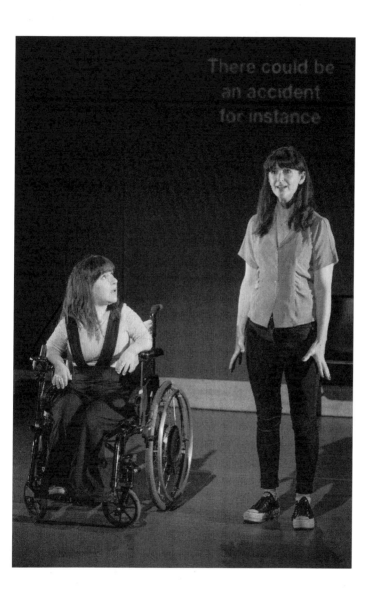

Characters

LISA
a four-foot-tall wheelchair user

RACHAEL
a non-disabled woman

Various members of the public, interviewed and recorded with their permission – their voices are heard and their words are seen projected onto the set.

The voices of four disabled showbiz friends who are:

Mat Fraser

Liz Carr

Cherylee Houston

Simon Startin

NOTES

This text has been assembled while we are still performing the show, so even though the piece will continue to evolve, what follows is as accurate a representation of what happens onstage as we have at the moment.

Rather than dividing the text into numbered Acts and Scenes we have kept titles for each section or scene, as this better represents how we put the piece together and how we refer to the different parts of it.

Some of the words the audience hear are recordings of the general public who are responding to questions put to them by Lisa and Rachael. These are represented in bold:

I think it could be about…erm…a friendship Maybe an unlikely friendship

When the audience hear these recordings the words spoken are projected onto the back wall of the set.

The other voice the audience hear is the Handsome Doctor in 'Goosechase 1.' These lines are recorded by a (handsome sounding) actor.

The set is a plain room that suggests, but not definitively, a rehearsal room. In it is a table, on which are a few of the props that will be used during the show. There is also a small and quite cheap looking electronic piano keyboard, an empty picture frame big enough to show the head and shoulders of someone and two chairs – one normal size and one with the legs cut down to make it very low to the ground.

RELAXED PERFORMANCE CHAT

RACHAEL: Hello.

LISA: Hello.

RACHAEL: I'm Rachael.

LISA: I'm Lisa.

RACHAEL: It hasn't started yet.

LISA: But when it does it'll be a lot like this.

RACHAEL: We just wanted to say that we would like you to respond to the show in any way you want to.

LISA: If you need to leave the auditorium at any point please do and come back whenever you're ready.

The lights close down to something more focused around them.

VOX POPS

RACHAEL: It all began when we decided we wanted to make a show together.

LISA: But we didn't have any ideas.

RACHAEL: So we went out and about and asked the public for theirs.

LISA: We said, 'Take a good look at us. What sort of play would we be in?'

RACHAEL: If you imagined two actors like us in a show, what sort of show do you imagine? What sort of characters do you imagine we would play?

LISA: What would the story be? What would the relationship be between us?

1

RACHAEL: And this is what they said…

They have MP3 players with them and put the buds in their ears.

They check in with each other that they are both ready, and with a synchronized gesture, they press 'play.'

RACHAEL and LISA speak the words they hear through their headphones.

ANT AND DEC

RACHAEL: There might be lots of um's and ah's. Ummm. When you say double act, you always tend to think a comedy double act like Morecambe and Wise, Ant and Dec that type of thing because you get, you play off each other. So, whether you're good guy bad guy, straight guy, funny guy. Erm, you might be the funny guy. I think you're probably cheeky. I don't know you've just got a cheeky face. Uhhhh, probably to try not make it part of the story cause otherwise it differentiates you. So you are, y'know, you're a wheelchair user, but why should that make you different? I don't know.

GRAB MY EYE

LISA: You definitely grab my attention and you grab my attention as well.

RACHAEL: Yeah, yeah but what as? I could see you playing Cinderella you know.

LISA: Like

RACHAEL: Cinderella. You know in one of those Disney… films/I could see you being in one of those, white dress, swirling around on ice or something like that. I don't know why.

LISA: I could see you being a funny kind of character, like not sneaky but like cocky and stuff like that. And I could see her being a very pleasant like character. Umm, like she could be umm/ yeah, the opposite of what you are.

RACHAEL: Opposite of you.

LISA: Something that will grab umm, people's eyes.

RACHAEL: Young minds attention.

LISA: Yeah cause I did say she would be a cocky kind of character. Kinda cheeky at times.

RACHAEL: No, I think you ought to be sisters always arguing or something like that/ That's what I think. Opposite sisters. Something that someone one gets more attention than the other.

LISA: No. No. No.

RACHAEL: Have you seen *Sister Sister*? Haven't you?/ Haven't you seen *Sister Sister* on Nickelodeon? It's a twins kind of show. It's like a twins show.

LISA: You need to watch that. Trust me.

LISA: Not everyone watches that. Put some kids in it as well. That would really grab people's eyes. You're writing the play, you'd be the main characters. And then maybe a male. A very strong./ Donominante. A very strong minded person like he could like it could like be something that happens nowadays he could maybe hit his wife./ or something like that.

RACHAEL: Tall, Tyreece, dark skin.

RACHAEL: Yeah that's what I was gonna say.

LISA: That wife.

RACHAEL: I think you're fighting over him. Nah, I think it should be more like you're not sisters exactly but one of you should be like the one that goes, that's with the man and then like he abuses that one of you and then one of you kinda like backs her up and one of you is always fighting with the man and so they don't like each other and you're not allowed round the house or whatever. And then like, what she, or whoever's playing the girlfriend or whatever, she doesn't like the fact that you don't like the boy so like you're always having arguments as well and then you kind of your friendship or sisterhood kind of like.......

LISA: Funny characters. To grab people's attention./Funny.

RACHAEL: Get Beyoncé in there. Trust me, you'll have millions.

LISA: You can't do that.

RACHAEL: Beyoncé. Yeah I know I'm just sayin. You can, that can happen you know. You can get Beyoncé.

LISA: In a film. Beyoncé don't do theatre. She does films.

RACHAEL: So you don't know. As long as she's getting paid she doesn't mind what she's doing.

OBSERVATIONS ON LIFE

RACHAEL: Are you gonna write it yourself? So you're very dialogue driven then rather than action? Are you good at observing people? I can see you in a small theatre set up to start off with. Doing something to do with observations with life. Have you got sort of a selection of people that you could call on? But not a cast of thousands? You clearly haven't got... y'know, maybe the resources for a cast of thousands. You never know. You might get people to come in... free. Maybe the best way to start without being too overly ambitious about it is to chose something where you can pick up on those observations and then you maybe embroider or elaborate on them. Telling your stories and anecdotes. You've probably got some very good stories that you could tell but you're not telling anything now!

SERIOUS PLAY

LISA: I suppose a serious play I would say. Yeah, yeah, yeah, yeah. A serious play…Ahhh. I can't, I just can't imagine two women doing a comedy. If I saw two women come on stage. I'd say a serious play.

LOT OF PLUCK

LISA: Drama? Drama? Are you going to do a drama of some sort? How many of you? Just the two of you?! I say, that's, that's, very enterprising, isn't it? Yes, you need a lot of courage, pluck for that, don't you think? Comedy would actually be very nice because you, you, you look to me as you could be very very funny. You know, you've got a smiley, happy, bright face, you know?

Yeah comedy. I would have thought you've got that sort of cheeky little face hasn't she? What do you think? Cheeky smile and lovely happy face.Well, Rachael could be your kind of straight person or something. Although, would you find that boring? I think comedy…because look as though you're very sparky and I'm not saying Rachael isn't as sparky but you've got that, as I said before she's got a sort of bright, sparky little cheeky face, hasn't she? Do you agree with me? Look at that. She's laughing at herself. She's funny. I'm sure she is. Don't give up. All the very best. I hope you get some better ideas.

RACHAEL: Can I just finish off the story I was just telling my friend? What was it?

LISA: About James and the –

RACHAEL: Oh yeah, yeah.

LISA: And the obsessions.

RACHAEL: I've got an autistic son. And he got very blokey with James.

LISA: That's right, yeah.

RACHAEL: And she rang up and she said right we'll report that. I know! Okay, I'm free.

LISA: We're free. What's this for? Oh right, so what you want to be girls?

RACHAEL: You should be the cheeky

LISA: Well, the Artful Dodger I was gonna say… the modern day Artful Dodger *(She laughs.)*

RACHAEL: And um I think you should encourage her to be cheeky. Yeah, I think, you know, lead from behind.

LISA: Does it have to be at this era or any era?

RACHAEL: Cheeky! Cockneys!/Cos that's where we come from. Don't we, umm

LISA: Well, like the old Dickensian bloke, you know, Oliver Twist, guy.

RACHAEL: Yeah. Be mischievous and adventurous and fun. Don't be boring. No, don't think you need to/ d'you know Lisa, when I was young, umm, it was the era when people had polio and there were no special schools and I can remember people being at school who had crutches and things like that. And we didn't have that emphasis on disability/ Now having said that, I've got a very difficult autistic son. And two, ord...normal daughters. He should have never gone to normal school. He created havoc wherever he went. Still does doesn't he?/ But you, there's nothing wrong with you in any way shape or form and people should just accept you/ for who you are... And and, I just feel so strongly about it, don't I?/ And so I would if anything I would make you the leader, with you, leading, pushing her to be the leader, so that people didn't see that you were smaller

LISA: We are much better at that sort of thing now in London aren't we.

LISA: Yeah, we are much better now than we were.

LISA: Yeah.

LISA: That's right, as you are.

LISA: Yeah.

LISA: Cause they aren't people like that who are there a lot of that and which they do, don't they? And poor little me films. So they don't want to... you don't want to that.

RACHAEL: No, no, don't even mention the disability. It's what you say and do –

LISA: That makes such power to the people whatever you are.

RACHAEL: Total yeah, talking about disability all the time and I actually said we've got look at a different way. We've got to look at the ability – what people can do not what they can't do.

They take the buds out of their ears.

LISA: Lots of ideas!

RACHAEL: Loads of ideas from the public.

LISA: They were very helpful weren't they.

RACHAEL: Very useful! Shall we try them out?

LISA: See which one's got legs.

RACHAEL: Which idea would be good for a whole show.

LISA: What did the first woman say?

RACHAEL: She talked about double acts. You'd be the funny one and that you had a cheeky face and I'd be the straight one.

LISA: But she didn't suggest a story so let's bear that in mind as a style. The 'Grab my eye!' Girls were next.

RACHAEL: 'Sister Sister'.

LISA: They talked about a domestic violence scene.

RACHAEL: Like what happens nowadays.

RACHAEL and LISA have already started setting up the stage for this scene, setting a chair SL.

LISA: Who's going to play the abused woman?

RACHAEL: They were looking at me when they said it.

LISA: You do look like a victim.

RACHAEL: I could use this small victim's chair.

RACHAEL sits in the chair.

LISA: Hang on a minute. What about the man? Who's going to play him?

RACHAEL: He'll have to be an unseen male presence. Like in 'The House of Bernarda Alba' Pepe al Romano.

LISA: Pepe El Romano? OK. Let's give it a go.

They pause for a second to ready themselves for the scene.

The lights change.

DOMESTIC ABUSE

Suddenly RACHAEL bursts into tears.

LISA: I've had enough of this Michelle! He's done this to you once too often. Look at your eye!

RACHAEL: I walked into the door.

LISA: You did not walk into the door. Don't give me that. I'm gonna get you some Savlon.

RACHAEL: But I love him.

LISA goes to fetch some Savlon. As she returns there is the sound of loud banging on a door.

RACHAEL: Oh my God! It's Pepe! *(Calling out.)* I love you Pepe!

LISA: Pepe! You can fuck off! Pepe El Romano? That's a wife beating name if ever I heard one.

RACHAEL: I've got no confidence.

LISA: I know. You haven't worn a scrap of make-up lately.

RACHAEL: I'm so unattractive. I need a make-over.

LISA: You need more than a makeover my girl you need to get yourself down the refuge. Or do you know what? This is going to come between you, me and your unborn child!

RACHAEL can keep a straight face no longer and they break out of it.

LISA: That was good.

RACHAEL: Very gritty.

LISA: I was actually going to give you a slap.

RACHAEL: I thought you were going to grab my eye. I don't know if I could do a whole show of that. Too emotional.

LISA: OK what was next?

RACHAEL: The woman who said we should do observations on life – two people and their observations.

LISA: Small theatre set up. Well this is perfect. *(Maybe mention the theatre they are in.)*

RACHAEL: Don't be overly ambitious.

LISA: You could get people to come in for free.

By now they have started to set up and sit on the chairs placed DSC.

OBSERVATIONS ON LIFE

BOTH: *(In unison.)* Observations on Life.

LISA: You got any observations Rach?

RACHAEL: I do, yes. I observe something to do with all this recording of people we've been doing. I observe that if we interview someone and they've got an accent – foreign or regional, or if they have a speech impediment or if they say inappropriate things, especially if it's about you, I find that quite thrilling. And then I feel a bit ashamed. I think I'm thrilled because I know it's like a way that I will get to say all those inappropriate things that I'm not usually allowed to say. It's a bit like the first audition bit of X Factor.

LISA: That's a good observation. Well done.

RACHAEL: Thank you. Do you have any observations?

LISA: I do yes. It's sort of connected to the interviews and how many people talked about my cheeky face.

RACHAEL: They did talk a lot about your cheeky face.

LISA: Yes. And it reminds me of something I call 'Here Comes Trouble Syndrome.' What that is, is when someone greets me, and it could be someone I've never met before but people I've known for quite a while do this as well, they have this way of greeting me which is… 'Here she comes! Here comes trouble!' and I….you can't really… how do you respond to that? Do you go *(imitating the way they were speaking)* 'Yes! Here I am!' or do you go *(very posh voice)* 'Good morning'…how do you start a conversation after that? I just don't know where to pitch it. So 'Cheeky Face' reminds me of 'Here Comes Trouble' That's my observation.

RACHAEL: Good observation.

BOTH: *(In unison.)* Observations on Life.

They stand up and move the chairs back to the US wall.

RACHAEL: Bit static.

LISA: You could get a lot off your chest in that show.

RACHAEL: Low budget. Be good for us.

LISA: Not sure it would sustain an entire evening.

RACHAEL: What was the next thing?

LISA: There was that bloke who said two women couldn't do comedy.

RACHAEL: Yes. If he saw two women it would be a serious play.

LISA: Well we definitely won't do a comedy then.

RACHAEL: After that was the women who kept going on about your cheeky face.

LISA: Bright, sparky, happy face.

RACHAEL: So we should do something about your cheeky face.

LISA: Then it was those two women who talked about me being a cheeky Cockney, modern day Artful Dodger.

RACHAEL: And I should encourage you to be cheeky. And she also said be mischievous, adventurous and fun. Don't be boring. This can mean only one thing, it's a number ladies and gentlemen.

RACHAEL gets the keyboard.

LISA puts on the top hat.

LISA: A cockernee style knees up. I've got this hat to help me with my character.

RACHAEL: And I'm in the background encouraging you to be the leader.

LISA: So people don't see that I'm smaller.

RACHAEL: Not sure I can achieve that. I'll give it a go. And I'm leading from behind so I should be on the piano.

LISA: Can you play the piano?

RACHAEL: No. Can you sing?

LISA: No.

CHEEKY FACE

RACHAEL begins to play and LISA does a song and dance number.

LISA: When skies are dark and cloudy and you're feeling mighty blue,
Don't worry chum coz here I come a'wheeling into view.
I may not be a normal member of the human race,
But then with glee you look and see my cheeky cheeky face.

Cheeky face.
Cheeky face.
There's never been,
Such a cheeky face.
When your sad,
Fings ain't so bad,
When you see me little cheeky face.

You start to think 'Don't cause a stink, show decorum and respect.'
You know it's key for you to be politically correct.
But ladies and gents of those sentiments there rarely is a trace
Because what pops right out your gob is 'Look at her cheeky face!'

Cheeky face.
Cheeky face.
There's never been,
Such a cheeky face.
Feeling crook?
Just take a look
At me lovely little cheeky face.

Their brain is frozen, no words get chosen, they don't wanna seem a fool.
How does it feel to move on wheels and be so miniscule?

They start to fidget, 'Dwarf or a midget in this particular case?'
Relieve the tension and only mention me cheeky cheeky
face!

Cheeky face.
Cheeky face.
There's never been,
Such a cheeky face.
It really doesn't matter
If I'm thin or I'm fatter,
Coz you only see me cheeky face.

RACHAEL: It's apparent I'm transparent when I'm standing
by the chair.
Lead from behind? They're being kind, it's like I'm just
not there.
But I'm not glum that my cheeky chum takes up all the
space.
Coz it's amazing what you can get away with,
When ya downstage of a cheeky face.

Cheeky face.
Cheeky face.
There's never been,
Such a cheeky face.
Next to her
I'm just a blur
In the shadow of her cheeky face.

LISA: See the smile on the pedophile when I walk into
the pub.
He'll be glad to pretend he's Dad as I give his knob a rub.
You may be shocked when I suck his cock or think it's a
disgrace,

But he's such a happy chappie when he comes on me
cheeky face.

Cheeky face.
Cheeky face.
There's never been,
Such a cheeky face.
If you're a perv,
I'm here to serve
You with me lovely little cheeky,
Forget the fact it's freaky,

RACHAEL: It's little and it's round and it's quite close to the
ground,

LISA: It's me lovely little cheeky face!

The song ends.

LISA: That has got legs!

RACHAEL: I'd enjoy doing a whole musical I don't think my
piano playing skills are up to it.

LISA: Or my singing.

RACHAEL maybe moves the keyboard back.

RACHAEL: Right then. Loads of ideas.

LISA: If you had to choose one to make into a show, which
one would you choose?

RACHAEL: No Idea. What about you?

LISA: No Idea.

RACHAEL: Yeah, we go shopping and then as a sort of by-product of the shopping, we might steal some stuff. Not big stuff. Like one way we do it is when we're picking stuff to try on, that all goes back on the wheelchair. Becomes like, it's really quite handy cause otherwise it gets quite heavy so everything goes on the back of there. Then it just becomes this massive pile of clothes. Plus you might pick up some earrings…

LISA: Knickers…

RACHAEL: Pants are good…

LISA: Socks, tea towels …

RACHAEL: And those just go there as small things and they go down the sides or …. and then sort of get forgotten about. A bit.

LISA: Yeah. Purses, sunglasses, bags, shoes. Flat shoes not high heels.

RACHAEL: I'll never steal shoes. I draw the line there.

LISA: The moral line?

RACHAEL: No, only because you can't steal a pair of shoes because they don't hang them out together.

LISA: They do in the kids section.

RACHAEL: But the other thing is with Lisa, even if they did think that you'd stolen a pair of earrings…

LISA: I could get away with that…

RACHAEL: They are never… Are they going to stop you after going out of the shop in your wheelchair? Probably not.

LISA: Well, I'd say that one, they'd never discover that I've stole it anyway cause I'm so good at stealing but if they happen to stop me then there's much more unlikely hood if I said 'Oh I forgot it was there' OR 'I forgot it was on the side of me' or even an up the sleeve factor I have is 'I can't feel my legs.' i.e. I couldn't feel that it was down there.

RACHAEL: And I would then go 'Don't – You can't ask...' Like, I'd step in as the person they'd want me to be which is like the carer.

LISA: You would go, 'Oh Lis, you can't get up. You're in pain. Aren't you?' Like that.

RACHAEL: 'You expect her to get up, look at her!' And then she'd go. *(LISA makes herself look ill and pathetic.)*

LISA: But all unspoken. Like we would never plan that. It's just what we know. Oh, and you never ever steal without buying something.

RACHAEL: No. That's one of the rules. Because one of the things that shopkeepers say is 'If someone buys something they probably not stealing.'

LISA: How wrong they are!

RACHAEL: It's worse for me to tell people that I shoplift than it is for you because for you, it's one of those typical things of they go 'Haha Lisa, oh what a one. Oh, trouble, here she comes, she shoplifts.'

LISA: In a wheelchair!

RACHAEL: They'd just find that hilarious. Hilarious. But for me, it's more sinister. It's like people go, 'You actually shoplift? You should know better.' It's the same as if you say outrageous sex stories about going to sex clubs and stuff they go 'Hahah' but if I say it, it's a bit more......

17

LISA: Real.

RACHAEL: 'Oh, you actually did that?'

LISA: It's like freaky girl does freaky things rather than normal girl does freaky things. It's different.

RACHAEL: Yeah.

LISA: It's more palatable. Like you're a bit weird anyway so the fact that you do weird things it's like by the by or something but with Rachael because she looks like butter doesn't melt in her mouth, you know like people get a bit like it's a bit left field for them sometimes. But she's actually worse than me.

RACHAEL: I am.

THE PACT

LISA: I have got an idea.

RACHAEL: Thank god for that.

LISA: This what we do. We ask the public the same question…

RACHAEL: If you imagine us in a show what would it be?

LISA: Yes. And we get the start of our story. Then we take that to someone else and ask them for the next part of the story.

RACHAEL: I get you, then ask someone else for the next part of the story…

LISA: So each person gives us the next little bit of the story. Like a game of consequences.

RACHAEL: Yes, but we have to take the first thing they say.

LISA: Are you sure? Because it's looking pretty good for me so far. I've got the lead role. I'm the funny one, the sparky one. I've definitely got the biggest part.

RACHAEL: I'm fine with that. I'm used to it. Small parts are what I usually get. Things like friendly nurse, saucy serving wench, supermarket Mum. I find it relieving anyway to have less to do. Less responsibility. I don't need any more responsibility in my life. Also with small parts you don't have to get so emotional. You can stay on the surface, you don't have to dig deep within your own personal trauma. If I want an emotional crisis I just go home.

LISA: I want to play something gritty, like one of them hard bitten cops who's an alcoholic or something... and a car chase, I'd love to do a car chase. Something that's not about disability, definitely.

RACHAEL: Anyway, whatever they say first of all we *have* to take?

LISA: Exactly. Let's make a pact.

RACHAEL: Let's shake on it

They shake hands.

GOOSECHASE 1

To the audience.

RACHAEL: So we went back to the public and asked the same question.

LISA: 'If you imagine us in a show, what would it be like? What would the show be about?'

I think it could be about erm...a friendship...maybe an unlikely friendship...

RACHAEL: We are friends in real life.

LISA: What makes for an unlikely friendship?

People with different personalities

LISA: OK. So what's Rachael like?

Shy. Introvert.

RACHAEL: 'In the background, leading from behind.'

LISA: 'Little bit boring.'

RACHAEL: Much as expected. And what about Lisa?

Bubbly. Yea. Very Bubbly

LISA: 'Sparky, bright.'

RACHAEL: 'Cheeky face.'

LISA: Maybe there's another reason that our friendship is an unlikely one?

One of you is really rich and the other one is not

LISA: One of us is really rich!

RACHAEL: Which one of us is the rich one?

You, coz you've got the wheelchair

LISA: Why would that make me rich?

If you were poor then it's going to make the audience like feel sorry for you

But if you're the rich one, then it's more equal kind of

LISA: So even if I'm a trillionaire I'll only ever be *kind of* equal to you.

RACHAEL: Yea, I think it's because even though I'm poor at least I'm normal.

LISA: Fair enough. What's the first thing that actually happens in the story?

There could be an accident for instance

BOTH: Oooh!

Like a street accident. Supposing you've just like me got a wonky knee, and you fell down

LISA: That's amazing! I have, actually, in real life, got two wonky knees.

RACHAEL: Which one of us would have the accident?

I think you

RACHAEL: *(RACHAEL points to herself and LISA points to her as well.)* Me?

Yes, 'cause you're already in a wheelchair...don't want to wish you any worse

LISA: You found that hilarious.

RACHAEL: I found it thrilling.

LISA: Aaah. Bless her. She's only trying to protect me. Doesn't want to give me a double dose. Right then, let's do it. Let's start the story.

LISA wheels into the far USL corner of the stage.

RACHAEL does the accident, falling down centre stage with her wonky knee.

LISA: How'd it go?

RACHAEL: Quite well I think. I wonder what happens to me now?

They order the ambulance

And you're there for absolutely ages in A&E with some rather brisk, brusque nurse pushing you round

RACHAEL goes over to get LISA's wheelchair

RACHAEL: I'm in A&E being pushed around, I need your wheelchair. *(She sits in the chair and wheels a little way.)* If I do some acting in this I might get an award.

RACHAEL wheels across the stage.

RACHAEL: Do you mind? Could you be a bit more gentle, I've just hurt my leg. You're being a bit brisk and brusque.

and then you're getting distressed and you sit there sobbing

RACHAEL sobs.

and there's this wonderful doctor comes along and sees this lovely young girl and you say 'I've been here for three hours and nobody's taken any notice of me'

RACHAEL: *(Sobbing.)* I've been here for three hours and nobody's taken any notice of me.

whisks you off into a cubicle

RACHAEL: I'm being whisked off to a cubicle by a *wonderful* doctor.

LISA: If he's going to examine you, I hope you've got clean knickers on.

RACHAEL: I hope I've got *some* knickers on.

RACHAEL puts her leg up.

22

He just tells her and now I will take care about you Mary

DR. V/O: And now I will take care about you Mary.

Because he knows her name.

RACHAEL reacts to this.

He says an important detail about her

RACHAEL moves her leg as if it is being examined by the doctor

DR. V/O: I know that you need your leg because you are a dancer.

She says why he knows this

RACHAEL: Why he knows this?

He asks her to go out for coffee and things like that

RACHAEL: Ummm

Not, no I wouldn't no

RACHAEL: *(Cheery.)* No thanks.

Because she's a bit afraid

RACHAEL: *(Afraid.)* No thanks.

Blackout.

I personally think she would speak to her friend

LISA: Come to my luxury apartment for some advice. *(RACHAEL gives LISA her wheelchair back.)* Yeah, I need that as that's what makes me rich.

RACHAEL goes and sits by LISA.

They would work out whether this bloke is a bit of a psycho or not

RACHAEL stands up and starts doing dance moves as she speaks.

RACHAEL: It's weird isn't it? I mean he's lovely but he knows my name…and that I'm a dancer…

Look I've got a friend he's a C.S.I chap

She gets the guy to tail the doc

LISA: *(Speaking into a phone.)* Hello, *(to RACHAEL)* my friend is a CSI chap. *(Back to phone.)* Yea, my friend Mary the dancer wants to go out with this hot doctor but he might be a psycho. Could you tail him for me and find out. OK Brilliant. *(Hangs up.)*

RACHAEL: What did he say?

LISA: He'll ring me back.

LISA's phone rings. She answers it.

They realised the doc actually was a friend of your sister

LISA: Oh he is a friend of your sister…!

RACHAEL: That explains everything. *(She gets a pashmina from the table and wraps it around herself.)* I'll definitely go out with him.

Blackout. RACHAEL sets up a chair CS and sits in it.

LISA: *(Still speaking into the phone.)* How are you doing babes? Haven't spoken to you in ages. Saw your Mum the other day up the market. Yea, you know that place there…

As soon as RACHAEL is settled in her chair…

RACHAEL: Lisa, the public didn't say any of that so it shouldn't be in the scene.

LISA: Oh.

You guys are in a restaurant. Wine and dine

RACHAEL: Ha ha ha ha. I love medical humor. I've had such a lovely evening, thank you. *(Waiter brings bill.)* No let's split it. Are you sure? It's a bit old-fashioned but I like it.

RACHAEL and the doctor walk out of restaurant.

They do lots of things you know walk along the street which is like its snowing and autumn, and yeah yeah that kind of stuff

RACHAEL: Like a montage?

Yeah.

RACHAEL: We could get a cab, but although it's autumn, I think it might snow, so let's walk.

Music. 'Arthur's Theme' by Christopher Cross.

RACHAEL does a montage of romantic moments: Caught in the rain, photo booth, summer picnic, roller coaster, snowball fight, slow dance. She then does a dance sequence.

He could meet the family

RACHAEL chucks her pashmina over LISA's face.

RACHAEL: Don't worry, you'll be fine, they'll love you.

RACHAEL: Hiya! Mum, Dad this is the Doctor. Not that Doctor.

DR. V/O: Hi.

RACHAEL: This is my sister.

DR. V/O: Oh…er… Hi.

Sister has a breakdown

RACHAEL: Sis? I better go see what's wrong.

Maybe there was history between her and the doctor going back some time, sexual history

RACHAEL: Right.

It would not be cool if you brought home your boyfriend and your sister went, 'Oh my God…ten years ago, banging his brains out.'

RACHAEL: Banging his brains out?

Threatens the sister to one side and just puts her straight. This guy that you love. I don't want you to see him again.

RACHAEL: How dare you threaten me to one side and put me straight. I love this guy. How can you ask me not to see him again?

RACHAEL on imaginary phone.

RACHAEL: The thing is Lisa, I feel so torn. So conflicted. I don't know what to do. On the one hand is my sister, who I love and on the other a wonderful doctor who I am in love with, who may one day be the father of my children. To be honest this is something that your money can't help me with. I'd love to come round and talk about it but there's so much happening in my life right now I don't think I have the time, you have no idea what a whirlwind of emotion this has been for me…

When RACHAEL starts talking on the phone LISA realizes that she is not in the scene. She walks over to RACHAEL and tries to get her attention. At some point during the above speech RACHAEL breaks off from her conversation to say to LISA something like

RACHAEL: Do you mind? I'm on the phone to my friend Lisa.

Then she carries on talking.

LISA turns away nonplussed then heads back to her wheelchair.

26

RACHAEL finishes with:

RACHAEL: I just don't know what's going to happen.

Blackout.

I'd have the sister disappear.

Lights up on RACHAEL facing US.

RACHAEL: Sister? Sister? Sister Sister!

Blackout.

The police would probably be very unhelpful and say wait forty-eight hours

She thinks 'I can't wait, so I'm going to have to start looking now'

RACHAEL: If you won't do anything, then I'll look for her!

RACHAEL storms out of the police station heading SR.

LISA: She would look?

Yea yea

Or both of you maybe? I dunno

Maybe split up and go different ways to look for her maybe?

LISA zooms enthusiastically to the middle of the stage beside RACHAEL.

LISA: So, split up and look for your sister!

RACHAEL: I think you just interfered with the story.

LISA: No I didn't.

RACHAEL: You did! When he said that I would go looking for my sister you said '*She* would look?' in a rather pointed way and then glared at him until he realized *you* wanted something to do so he said we should split up and both look for her.

LISA: Well if we are going to pull on that string, when that Kiwi lady talked about those little scenes and you said 'What like a *montage*?' And that's not interfering with the story?

RACHAEL: She meant montage but she just couldn't think of the word.

LISA: So we split up to look for your sister?

RACHAEL: He only says maybe we do.

I think they'd split up to look for them

LISA: So what would Rachael do?

Ask the doctor to help find her

RACHAEL: And what about Lisa?

You could like call one of your like secret undercover agents and then your undercover agents could like help on it like start looking undercover

LISA zooms backwards to the corner where she has spent the whole scene.

LISA: So I get to make another phone call?

RACHAEL: Yea.

LISA leaves the stage…

REHEARSAL ROOM CHAT

LISA: I'm not doing it.

RACHAEL: What? What do you mean? What about the pact?

LISA: I haven't even left my luxury apartment!

RACHAEL: That's the risk when you ask the public and you make a pact.

LISA: That's what I'm regretting.

RACHAEL: Because you're not in it?

LISA: Yea.

RACHAEL: So you thought it was fine when you thought you were going to get the main part and I would not get much to do but now it has gone the other way the pact is not a good idea any more.

LISA: Exactly. Although you were great. You had a romantic montage with a hot doctor...

RACHAEL: I was the main part. That never happens. It was very unexpected because they said I would be in the background, the shy introvert leading from behind. It was opposite of what they said.

LISA: In the first set of interviews they said I would be the lead part, the funny one, but when we asked them to write an actual story they didn't even put me in it. I observe how familiar that feels....Like with men, they say 'Oh you're a great catch, you're intelligent, you're funny, you cook a great risotto...'

RACHAEL: You do.

LISA: It's leaving it. That's the thing with risotto. If I like them I might say 'Do you fancy going for a drink?' and they go 'Not me! I wasn't talking about me! I meant you're a great catch for somebody else, not me!' What they say and what they do. We all know we should live in a world that is more equal and everything but when it comes to it, no one wants to actually do anything. Same thing.

RACHAEL: It's a bit depressing.

LISA: It is a bit depressing.

US 2 – WOW FACTOR

LISA: We call it the WOW factor.

RACHAEL: It's when you wow someone off. It happens to this friend if ours all the time.

LISA: On special occasions he insists on wearing this cropped, patchwork leather jacket.

RACHAEL: In various shades of tan, that he thinks is really special.

LISA: People always go…

RACHAEL: WOW! Amazing jacket!

LISA: WOW! I've never seen anything like it!

RACHAEL: He think's that's good!

LISA: So he keeps wearing it.

RACHAEL: But that is not good. That is being WOWed off. I get it when I tell people I've three children. WOW! YOU'VE GOT THREE CHILDREN! YOU! What they mean is, three is NOT GOOD! Why would you do that? Two, good. Three, not good. Which is true. Three is stupid. I realise that now, but it's not the sort of thing you can test out.

LISA: I get the getting out of the wheelchair WOW. It happens all the time but it happened recently when I went for a massage and I was explaining that I could get out of my chair to get on the table, and as I was demonstrating the therapist said, WOW! WOW! OH WOW! And that just carried on throughout the whole treatment. So relaxing.

RACHAEL: Everyone's got their own WOW.

LISA: Watch out for the WOW.

REHEARSAL ROOM CHAT

RACHAEL: So what are we going to do?

LISA: We still need a story. Asking the public didn't work.

RACHAEL: Yes it did they came up with a really good story.

LISA: For you!

RACHAEL: Well you do it then, you make something up.

LISA: I haven't got any ideas.

RACHAEL: Well you know what they say?

LISA: What?

RACHAEL: Write what you know. That's what everyone does anyway. They might say it's not about them, but everyone knows it is really. So it should be about an actress called Lisa.

LISA: I don't want to play myself.

RACHAEL: It's not you, it's a version of you. It might look like you. It might sound like you. but isn't you.

THE STORY OF LISA THE ACTRESS

LISA plays herself. RACHAEL plays all the other characters.

NARRATOR: Once upon a time there was an actress called Lisa. She was often out of work and poor, struggling to make ends meet. One day she was out shoplifting for essential items: vitamins, sanitary towels, luxury crabmeat, when she got a phone call from her agent.

LISA's mobile phone rings.

AGENT: Hello darling. How are you? Audition for a telly job darling. Regular role on a well established continuing drama. And darling, not a disabled part.

LISA: *(To audience.)* In my real life, a non-disabled role would be great because I have to do 'disability' all the time, like it's the only interesting thing about me, but a non-disabled role means I can be in a story that could happen to any of you.

NARRATOR: The next morning Lisa went to meet the casting director.

C.D.: Hi Lisa! Thanks for coming in. I've always thought you would be so right for this show and when I saw the breakdown for a sparky, cheeky cockney I immediately thought of you! and...it's not a disabled part. Good luck!

LISA's mobile phone rings.

AGENT: Hello darling. You've got the job.

NARRATOR: The big day came. The first person she met was the studio manager.

S.M.: Welcome to the studios. This will be your home from now on. And this is your dressing room. *(Opens door and slams it shut.)* This is a different world Lisa. And different rules apply. From this day forth your life will never be the same. Now tell me Lisa, are there any skeletons in your closet? Because if there are, they will come out and be all over the papers.

LISA: Umm, no I don't think so.

S.M.: Good. Luck.

LISA: *(To audience.)* In my real life, if it was in the tabloids that I'd been rogered up the alleyway by a Premiership footballer or caught snorting cocaine off a stripper's tits, I think that would be *good* for disability because it's always about Pudsey Bear and inspiration isn't it? Bollocks to all that, let's rock it up a bit.

NARRATOR: Then it was time to meet the writer.

WRITER: If you could imagine yourself in a story, what sort of story do you imagine? What do you think a story with someone like you in it might be about? What sort of character would you play?

LISA: I'm excited to be in the stories that you are going to think up. Everything this show is famous for. All the crying, the shouting, the domestic abuse.

WRITER: So what are the practicalities of you and your wheelchair?

LISA: I use the chair because I get chronic pain.

LISA gets out of the chair.

WRITER: Wow!!

LISA: With me you get two for the price of one. A walker and a sitter.

WRITER: Wow. This is great news! Because we were thinking you could only be friends with the characters who had accessible houses but this opens up so many other options! What do you do with your chair when you go somewhere that isn't accessible?

LISA: I leave the chair outside.

WRITER: Wow! Great. Does it not get stolen?

LISA: The only time it got stolen was at Disneyland. Me and my family came off a ride and it was gone.

WRITER: Ha! Brilliant! That gives me a really good idea! You could go to say, Jack's house, and leave your chair outside and then the gang could steal it from outside and take it all round the square and then in and out of the market and ride it to the tube station and then you see your chair going down the escalators, bumping down the stairs and then you could see your chair have a whole like London montage, going to all the sights: St. Pauls, Houses of Parliament, Big Ben, and you could see your chair going on this big adventure! That would be so funny!

LISA: Just to say…that's a story for the wheelchair.

NARRATOR: Lisa's final meeting of the day was with the Boss.

BOSS: Got big plans for you. Big plans. This is going to be exciting. Exciting for us, exciting for you, exciting for the viewer. How are you feeling? Excited?

LISA: I'm really excited. I'm hoping we can do something different with this.

BOSS: I know what you're saying. One hundred percent. This is a non-disabled part. We want to do something unprecedented. And, this is going to sound clichéd, but I think we're going to change the world with this.

NARRATOR: At that moment something in her changed. Lisa went home full of hope.

LISA: Dear Diary…… Oh I've had a lovely day at the studios. I can't wait to get started. When the Boss said to me about changing the world, I got really excited. I think he could be right. Me playing a non-disabled part, being on telly all the time, in people's living rooms week after week, I think we can change the world. Better get to sleep. Early starts from now on. After all, my life will never be the same again.

She falls asleep.

AN ACTRESS NONTAGE

A sequence of short scenes in which the characters other than LISA are not seen but are voiced by RACHAEL.

The alarm sounds. LISA turns it off. We hear 'Work' by Rihanna.

DJ: Goooood morning London, it's 5am. Rise and shine. Let's get to work!

LISA wakes and stretches. It is very early.

She steps away from her bed. Jump cut to her doing Tai chi.

Jump cut to her in her car.

LISA: Alright Jim, how's the traffic this morning?

DRIVER: Not too bad. Got you your regular smoothie with a little wheatgrass for energy.

LISA: Aw thanks babe you're a sweetheart. Can't talk darlin' gotta learn me lines.

She opens her script and finds her lines.

LISA: 'I said I'd meet you in the pub alright?!'

She flicks through the rest of the script but she has no more lines. She is fine with that.

Jump cut to her arriving at the studio and saying hello to all her actor mates.

ACTRESS: Alright darlin, early start ain't it?

LISA: Yeah I'm still in my onesie!

ACTRESS: I know, you never get used to these early starts.

LISA: See you on set later.

Jump cut to her in the make-up chair.

MAKE-UP: Just popping an eye drop in. I've got a lovely new mascara I want to try out on you. Very lengthening.

LISA: Oh how lovely. How's your husband?

MAKE-UP: Oh he's alright. Thank you so much for asking. That's very sweet of you.

LISA is called onto the set.

1ST AD: Ready for you on set Lisa.

LISA: Coming.

LISA is on set. She finds her mark. The 'about to do a take' warning bell sounds.

1ST AD: Running up to speed. Action.

LISA: *(Very dramatic.)* 'I said I'd meet you in the pub later alright?!'

1ST AD: And cut.

Bell sounds again.

Marvellous Lisa, thank you. That's you wrapped for the day.

LISA saying goodbye to everyone.

ACTRESS: Oh bye babe.

LISA: See you at the awards tonight, what you wearing?

ACTRESS: Not sure. I've got a choice of two. I'll whatsapp you.

Jump cut to LISA on the red carpet doing lots of glamorous posing with the paps calling out to her.

PAPS: Lisa, Lisa, Over here! Just one more Lis. Top right, top right. That's lovely…

LISA: Alright Bob! I've gotta go, I've gotta go in, I'll see you later.

Jump cut to her in the party talking to another actress.

LISA: Congratulations on your award for Best Actress. You really deserve it.

ACTRESS: Oh, thank you. Next year it'll be you. One good story and you'll be picking this up. I think what you're doing on the show is great. You're a breath of fresh air. What you're doing is really important.

Jump cut to her hailing a taxi.

LISA: Taxi!

Jump cut to her in front of her mirror taking off her make-up. She hears the echoing voices of people saying how important this is going to be for her and for the world.

ECHO V/O: 'What you're doing is so important...'

'We are going to change the world with this...'

'Snorting cocaine off a stripper's tits...'

THE STEPS DOWN TO LEAVING THE SHOW

At the end of each interaction LISA does a little circle in her chair coming straight back for the next time she and the BOSS meet.

NARRATOR: Lisa the actress was filming her scenes, doing her job and waiting for the story that would come her way. But the days turned to weeks and the weeks turned to months. She was sure there would be a story and so she went to see the Boss to find out what it might be.

BOSS: Hi Lisa.

LISA: I've been on the show five months. I'm settling in and loving it. I just wondered what might I have coming up? Story-wise?

BOSS: You know what Lisa? I'm so proud of this show. It's ensemble. Everyone gets their time in the light. Granted, you're out of the light at the moment, but you know, we've got big plans. Huge plans for you. Massive.

LISA does a circle.

LISA: I've been here for nearly a year now. I had those few scenes here and there but I was wondering…

BOSS: I hear you, I hear you, and you're absolutely right. And do you know what? Er…I'm ashamed to say, it's the writer. They keep giving me stories about disability and I know you don't want that so I say 'No. No. No.' But they just keep coming back with these medical, disability storylines and, quite rightly, that's not for you. But don't worry. I've got plans. Big plans. Yea?

LISA does a circle.

A section where LISA tries to say something but the BOSS keeps her quiet by interrupting with positive sounding phrases.

LISA: I just wanted…

BOSS: I know, I know.

LISA: No it's…

BOSS: I hear you. Absolutely. I know.

Etc.

LISA does a circle.

LISA: I've been here nearly two years and still no story.

BOSS: Granted that cast member unexpectedly left and your stories may have been connected to them, there's been movement in the team at the top and that created its own difficulties. And then we had to do Christmas and that put everything back. Then of course… Brexit. That has definitely caused disruption.

LISA does a circle.

During this section there is a game where the BOSS keeps trying to interrupt LISA but LISA shuts her up by lifting her finger to the BOSS.

LISA: I've been here two and a half years now. I've been doing some work on trying to figure out why I haven't had a story. I thought maybe it was because I wasn't a good enough actor to carry a story, so I asked people what they think: directors, other actors…

BOSS: We certainly don't think that. We brought you in because we think you are a terrific actor.

LISA: Then I wondered if it was a scheduling issue. Whether worries about whether I could carry that workload were getting in the way, so I spoke to scheduling and they said 'no,' that wasn't a concern. I've looked at the actors who joined at the same time as me, and the ones who joined a little while after me and I wrote down all the storylines they had and the contrast is remarkable. I think there's a problem. A problem writing for me.

Change of atmosphere.

BOSS: There is no problem.

LISA: I can help you. Write a story for another character and then put my name on it. It'll get you past the problem.

BOSS: But there is no problem.

LISA: There is no problem?

BOSS: No.

LISA: Please…when you say there is no problem it makes me feel like I'm a bit mad because it seems so clear to me and yet everyone is behaving like it's all OK.

BOSS: I hear you, I hear you. But if there's no problem, there's no problem.

LISA does a circle.

LISA: I've been here four years now and I genuinely wonder whether anything can be done about this. You know my frustrations.

BOSS: OK. OK. Stories right? Stories. Let's think of something right now. It could be to do with the market, with your family, I know, I know, your mother. Your real…your birth mother…you search for your birth mother. Yea?

LISA: OK. That sounds like…

BOSS: Good story? Yea.

LISA: Yea.

BOSS: Who could play your mother? Who is going to play that? I know. Not the mother, the father. You go looking for your birth father. Yea? You with me on this? Because… perfect person to play your father…

LISA: Who?

BOSS: Warwick Davis.

Brilliant. Warwick fucking Davis.

LISA does a circle but this time she comes back she stops, facing us, beside RACHAEL.

Changing the world Lisa, one dwarf at a time.

Presses button on an intercom on his desk.

Susan. Get me Warwick Davis.

Warwick, it's me. I've got plans. Huge plans.

LISA: That was that. I knew I couldn't change the world.

REHEARSAL ROOM CHAT

LISA: Well that didn't work.

RACHAEL: I can't believe you didn't get a story. When did you actually start that TV job…?

LISA: Fictional job.

RACHAEL: When did you start that fictional job?

LISA: Nearly five years ago.

RACHAEL: And when the public made up that other story about Mary the dancer, the one you weren't in, when was that?

LISA: Nine years ago. I know where you are going with this…

RACHAEL: I bet things have changed since then. What with all the inclusivity, equality…

LISA: Yeah, there's diversity, panel debates, there are 'agents for change' these days…

RACHAEL: There's one-armed CBBs presenters now and *Strictly* is very diverse, it's happening out there

LISA: I think you might be right.

RACHAEL: We should go back out and ask the public the same question. I bet you it'll be different.

LISA: OK!

RACHAEL: Let's do it! So we asked the public the same question:

LISA: If you could imagine us two in a show, what would the show be about?

I think you two erm look like you know each other since high school and you're like growing up friends

LISA: OK, we were friends in high school.

RACHAEL: I wonder why we were friends?

Ahhhh because your mums gave you the same bowl cut

LISA: OK, strong look the bowl cut.

RACHAEL: But why would that make us friends?

Because you went through such bullying with this one haircut that it bonded you for life.

RACHAEL: OK so we are both outsiders.

LISA: Living on the fringes of society.

She's the shy one and you're the mouthy one…

LISA: So you're shy and I'm mouthy. Classic.

RACHAEL: Exactly the same as before, me introvert and you cheeky face.

…ohhh she's hypnotized me with her eyes

LISA: What did you do with your eyes?

RACHAEL: Nothing. I just did this. *(Does a weird look with her eyes.)*

You both really like Marmite and someone near was having a loud conversation about how much they

**hate people who like Marmite and they were like...
you were like were like fighting the Marmite cause
and that brought you together**

RACHAEL: Ooh, so we're Marmite activist outcasts, rebels... I can relate to that.

LISA: So what's the first thing that happens in this story?

A death. That's always good.

RACHAEL: Death. Very dramatic.

LISA: Who dies?

**A friend of yours from school who you haven't
seen them for years and then you just hear on the
grapevine that they've died**

They separate ready to do the first scene. The sound of a doorbell.

LISA: Come in it's open.

RACHAEL: Hi.

LISA: I've done you some Marmite on toast.

RACHAEL: Oh lovely thanks. *(She takes the toast.)* Have you trimmed your hair?

LISA: Yea. Do you like it?

RACHAEL: Yea I'll do mine, pass the bowl.

LISA: Did you hear? A friend of ours from school...dead!

RACHAEL: How did you hear?

LISA: On the grapevine how else?

RACHAEL: It's usually through.

LISA: Well this time it was on.

43

RACHAEL: I wonder how they died?

They can't just die. I mean I've had school friends who've just died from cancer or whatever but there's not much of a story in that is there?

RACHAEL: I'm not sure a person with cancer would agree with that.

LISA: Very harsh.

You both receive the same letter from the friend

Another scene where RACHAEL goes round to LISA's house. Sound of a doorbell.

LISA: Come in it's open.

RACHAEL: Hi.

LISA: Hi. I've done you some Marmite on toast.

RACHAEL: Oh lovely thanks.

LISA: You're not going to believe this. I've received a letter from the friend.

RACHAEL: Oh my god. I received the same letter.

And then one of your school friends contacts you and says 'I've had this really odd letter'

RACHAEL: Which one of us do they contact?

You

RACHAEL: Me. OK.

Phone rings and RACHAEL answers it.

And she's saying this really odd letter has come from Anna, who's died.

RACHAEL: Oh yes. 'Anna.'

She said I have to come and see you because there's something that's...some information that we have to investigate

We hear a different doorbell and RACHAEL answers the door.

RACHAEL: Ah hello. Come in. I was just having a snack, I hope it doesn't offend you. Yes, don't think I've forgotten what you put me through all those years ago. Anyway, I'm sure we've all grown up since then. For some reason Anna has brought us together. And we need to find out why.

You've got to investigate the cause of the death

LISA: Who's going to investigate?

You

RACHAEL: Me?

Yea

LISA: OK. On her own...?

Of course

RACHAEL: What about this other friend who's come to see me?

Of course. And she could come to see you. You decide together

LISA: Rachael and this other friend, not me?

Yeah. So it's you and your friend that investigates the cause of the death.

LISA wheels herself into the corner

RACHAEL: Told you, you either love it or hate it. Sometimes you just have to try these things. OK. I think we're ready to put the past behind us and investigate this death together.

You go to Anna's house to find out whether you can get some evidence or find out about what happened to Anna

RACHAEL: But where shall we start? All I've got is this letter. It's got her address......Anna, The House on the Hill. Let's start there.

RACHAEL crosses the stage in dim and spooky lighting.

RACHAEL: Stick close to me friend. Don't worry, the Marmite sisterhood will protect us. There's the house!

You turn up to the door and

A loud burst of music. A jumpscare moment.

You see someone who evidently wasn't meant to be there maybe climbing out of the window – an intruder!

RACHAEL: An intruder! If we are going to find some evidence we need to go into the house.

RACHAEL squirts some smoke onto the stage. She (and friend) enter the house.

The police have some knowledge of the house because for years there has been talk of it being haunted

Huge clap of thunder and lightning. Ghostly wind. RACHAEL reacting as if bats are flying around her.

The history of the haunting goes back to where perhaps a ritual sacrifice took place

RACHAEL: Friend? Where are you? Don't leave me!

Horror movie atmosphere is really ramping up. RACHAEL is abandoned by the friend and ends up facing upstage. We also hear an echo version of 'Ooh she's hypnotising me with her eyes!'

Someone entering people's bodies and trying to make them do evil

RACHAEL turns downstage and start talking in a possessed 'Exorcist' style voice.

Had she been contacted through the spirit world to find out what had happened and someone is trying to stop her

Full-on scary sounds now with screams and ghostly whispering. A flaming pentagram appears on the back wall and drags RACHAEL back. She is pinned to the wall by an unseen force and her arms are spread either side of her as she twitches uncontrollably, possessed by the spirit of evil...

LISA: Stop! Stop!

RACHAEL: What you doing? I was getting into that.

LISA: It's happened again! I didn't even get a luxury apartment this time just this fucking letter.

What's going on? I thought it had changed? One-armed CBBs presenters and all that. Am I going mad or something? Have things got better for disabled people or not?

RACHAEL: Maybe it is just you? Maybe things are way better but...not for you.

LISA: Thanks very much.

In this scene we hear recordings of the voices of MAT, LIZ, CHEZ and SIMON but we don't see their words projected onto the back wall.

RACHAEL: You should ask your successful disabled showbiz friends. I bet they think things have got loads better.

LISA: OK. I will. What do you reckon Mat?

MAT V/O: **It's got better in so far as they're using us more to pepper the façade, to make it look like it is more equal than it really is but when it comes to having disabled actors within their character, which is under some kind of crisis, show the human condition, those are really not happening yet.**

LISA: Which is basically what I said right? Still not getting a story. Liz?

LIZ V/O: **I think there's always been disability on TV, more than we think. Whether it's *Crossroads*, or *El Dorado*, we forget that disability – stuff that you've been in Lisa, *Grange Hill*...**

LISA: *(To the audience.)* Yep. I was in *Grange Hill* for a couple of years

LIZ V/O: **So there's this kind of 'Oh things have changed and they're improved' I don't know that things are that different, I think we've always been there in the media but people don't see us wherever we are and whatever we do and I don't quite know why that is but we're invisible whether we're on TV or not.**

LISA: So Liz reckons even if we did get a story we'd still be invisible.

RACHAEL: And she definitely thinks things are no better.

LISA: Hi Chez.

CHEZ V/O: **Hello lovely.**

LISA: Has the world moved on?

CHEZ V/O: **No! The world hasn't moved on. The world keeps telling us it's moved on but it's gone backwards in a lot of ways I think.**

LISA: Really?

CHEZ V/O: **I think I get treated worse than I did ten years ago as a person with a disability, I think people understand us a lot less and yet there's a few more of us on the telly.**

RACHAEL: How's that happened?

CHEZ V/O: **I could give you a list but I don't think any of them are defining things: cutting care meaning a lot of people with disabilities fighting just for existence, you know – daily food and going to the loo and all that stuff and not being able to get into education, then you've got *Superhumans* on Channel 4...**

LISA: Yes. The bloody Paralympics. The number of people who assume I can swim because of Ellie Simmonds. Chuck me in a swimming pool I'd fucking drown.

CHEZ V/O: **I think I definitely get treated worse because of the perception that you're a scrounger or whatever if you're...when a guy saw me stand up out of my chair to transfer to another chair he shouted at me across from the bus stop then came and knocked on the door when I left and told Toby he was going to the papers because I was a benefit cheat. You know what I mean? That sort of perception is...is more rife. Coz yea, targeted abuse is up massively for disabled people.**

RACHAEL: That happens to you. Shouted at in the street.

LISA: And when I get out my chair on T.V, I get abused on Twitter. Simon?

SIMON V/O: **Have things got better really? There's a hideous kind of hall of mirrors that's been created and the little silver bauble of casting a disabled person on a soap and saying 'Look things are getting better' or giving us a scheme or giving us some Arts Council funding or whatever, it feels really churlish to say 'Oh that's horrible' because it's not horrible, it gets us to what we want to do but I can't help thinking that we're part of a Cripperatti, we're privileged, its corrupting us a little bit and and I don't think it's really serving the agenda of bringing us together very much.**

LISA: Because the Cripperatti are actually…

SIMON V/O: **Inspiration porn, which is sort of addressed with this lauding disabled people as heroes of discus and javelin and, you know, the superhuman narrative that Channel 4 foisted on us while Ian Duncan Smith was killing thousands of us.**

LISA: A group of successful, high achieving disabled people whether they're actors or athletes or whatever, them being really visible in the media actually makes it easier to let 'ordinary' disabled people die.

SIMON V/O: **People who've most suffered are people with learning impairments and people with depression and things like that who, you know, they've got a tendency to want to kill themselves at the best of times and then we just take away every means of them staying alive and say 'No, if we kick away your crutches you'll be stronger.' So they've**

sort of set up this game where if we kick away your crutches the more inspirational you'll become.

DWP STATS

Music.

Text appears on the back wall showing the names of people, their age and how they died because of benefit cuts or sanctions or other actions by the DWP.

When three stories have appeared and faded LISA and RACHAEL get the frame and begin to frame different parts of each other. LISA first – head, feet, hands front on, then, with her body turned away, her face looking back at us. Then RACHAEL head, feet, hands side on, her body turned away with her face looking back at us.

When they have done that they put the frame back and watch as the last 'page' of three names appears and fades.

US 3

RACHAEL: We can be together without doing anything.

LISA: Without speaking.

RACHAEL: People say, 'Smile, it doesn't cost you anything!'

LISA: But it does. It costs you big time.

RACHAEL: With us it doesn't cost us anything. It's no effort.

LISA: It's as good as being on your own but without the feeling lonely bit. We always say 'Well done' to each other.

RACHAEL: Yeah like we'll ask 'What did you do today?'

LISA: 'I just went to Sainsburys.'

RACHAEL: 'That it?'

LISA: 'Yeah.'

RACHAEL: 'Well done!'

LISA: We have the exactly same rhythm. That's why we
became friends.

RACHAEL: We were doing this job, touring the world, and
after the show every night, everyone else would be going,
'Tomorrow I'm gonna get up early, go for a run, have a
green smoothie,'

LISA: 'Get down Bondi, go surfing.'

RACHAEL: 'Climb the harbour bridge.'

LISA: And they'd go, 'What are you guys gonna do?'

RACHAEL: And we'd be like, 'Have a bagel, watch TV?'

LISA: 'Do the show.'

RACHAEL: 'Go to a sex club?' That's enough.

LISA: You can't do it all.

RACHAEL: Wouldn't want to.

REHEARSAL ROOM CHAT

LISA: You know what we are going to have to do don't you?

RACHAEL: No! Don't say those words.

LISA: Well an experiment is not a scientific if you only do it
twice. Rule of three.

RACHAEL: That's not a scientific rule that's a comedy rule.

LISA: A rule's a rule.

RACHAEL: OK. Maybe you're right. Remember what the
woman said in the first interviews?

LISA: What?

RACHAEL: Don't give up.

CRIP GC

I would say sisters. The first thing that came to mind was sisters.

LISA: Sisters. That makes sense.

RACHAEL: Sister Sister.

LISA: Some people do think we're sisters.

RACHAEL: Especially when we're wearing our glasses. *(They both put their glasses on.)*

I'd say you're the younger one and you're the older one

LISA: I'm the older one? How dare they?

Lisa's not quite as nice as what people think she is, but everybody loves Lisa first of all when they meet her

LISA: What's not to love?

and Rachael always gets into trouble because of Lisa

LISA: Ooh very complex.

RACHAEL: No mention of your cheeky face.

Lisa could give money to a homeless person

RACHAEL: That makes a change. They usually give money to you.

LISA acts out giving the homeless person some money.

LISA: There you go mate, keep the change, buy yourself a
Pret sandwich.

**He's selling Big Issues then he gets out a Big Issue
that's underneath his pile and hands it over to Lisa
that's got a stash of drugs in it.**

LISA goes back to the Big Issue seller and does the drug deal.

LISA: You got that special edition for me, keep it quiet yeah?
Cheers. Stay lucky Babes.

**And someone could come down and notices the
drugs but really is a policeman**

LISA: Ohh, alright mate?

**So you drop the magazine and Rachael picks it up,
obviously not knowing what's inside it**

LISA drops the magazine and RACHAEL picks it up

RACHAEL: Lisa, you've dropped your magazine.

**You're blatantly going to go 'I'm disabled, it's not
me' and blame your younger sister**

LISA: I'm disabled it's not me! *(Cries.)* Of course I'm not
buying drugs are you kidding me? I'm a nice person,
you've just met me and you love me don't you? If you
want to know what's going on then talk to her!

*LISA watches as the policeman crosses in front of her towards
RACHAEL.*

RACHAEL: Yes, can I help you officer?

**So you are able to distract the undercover policeman
Fall off...fall out of the wheelchair**

*LISA does an elaborate and attention-grabbing fall from her chair.
As soon as she is on the floor –*

Rachael would help you get up

RACHAEL: Sister! *(RACHAEL puts the magazine on the floor next to LISA.)*

LISA: Sister sister!

While you explain the situation about your sister to the undercover cop and what's wrong with her

RACHAEL: Oh no, you must be mistaken.

Out of the magazine, Lisa's put the drugs in Rachael's bag

LISA does that.

RACHAEL: You see not only is she very old, she is also having a polio flare-up.

Rachael works at the Houses of Parliament. Employees get searched and they search her bag and find the drugs and she gets suspended pending investigation

LISA wheels away. RACHAEL faces DS as if her bag has just been searched by security.

RACHAEL: I don't understand. I've never seen that before in my life.

The next scene would be Lisa in her workplace getting a phone call to say that you have been suspended.

LISA: Suspended pending investigation?

She's got to work out a way to help you

LISA: Don't worry. I'll figure out a way to help you. I've got this!

Lisa is an undercover cop working on a drugs bust. So then she's gonna have to go to her boss and explain what's happened.

LISA gets out of her chair DSC. Sound of a door slam.

LISA: What a cock up. Nineteen months' undercover work nearly blown by PC-fucking-Plod. Why weren't Uniform told to stay away from the Big Issue seller? I'm using him to get to the top man, Pepe El Romano but you fucked up big time. Or maybe you're on the take? Maybe you're in Pepe's pocket? Maybe you wanted my cover blown? Well now my sister's been suspended and I'm not happy which is bad news for you my son. You're going down!

LISA leaves the office. Sound of a door slam.

RACHAEL: Hey, this is going really well for you! I reckon you're gonna get a car chase in a minute!

LISA: Rule of three! Told you!

RACHAEL: Good job we didn't give up. Third time lucky.

LISA: Wasn't luck though was it?

RACHAEL: No. It wasn't to do with luck. It was because all the people who made up that last story were disabled.

LISA: They were all disabled.

RACHAEL: I think that's good. Very clear message from the show. Put disabled people into positions of power: writing the stories, commissioning, programming, and things will change. We've actually shown that, very unscientifically but still! Pretty good.

LISA: No. No... It's not good, it's not.

Just on a practical level – for disabled people to all get into those positions – when we so often struggle to get basic help to live, do you know how long that will take? I'll never see it in my lifetime. I don't want change 'for the children of our future' I want change for me now. It feels worse now than before, ten years ago everyone was in agreement that it was shit and the world wasn't ready to imagine stories with us in them – and however shit that felt – it made sense 'cause everyone could admit that. Nowadays it's like they all look at you and say 'You're visible, it's done…stop moaning' but it's so not done and it makes you feel like your going mad when you hear that because you know it's not the truth…

And worse than that? Those lovely, good, kind-hearted people who desperately want to believe that we should all be equal… I'm not in their stories. I'm not in the world that they imagine. It makes me feel not like you, something 'other', an alien. That's a lonely feeling.

The only thing I knew when we first started to make this was that I didn't want to make a show about disability, because that's the only thing people expect to see from me, and here I am doing exactly that. I do it too. Back to the only story I can tell…

'What's your idea?' I have no idea. I still have no idea. I only have, it would seem, this. I'm tired of it.

LISA has stood up out of her chair. She sinks to the floor.

After a moment RACHAEL sinks to the floor in the same way that LISA did and is lying beside her.

They look at each other and start to giggle.

They come up onto their elbows.

LISA: You can't do it all.

RACHAEL: Wouldn't want to.

BOTH: Well done!

FINALE SONG

LISA starts singing unaccompanied from the floor. Slowly she begins to get to her feet.

LISA: Cheeky Face, cheeky face,
    There's never been such a cheeky face.
    We're on the floor,
    Can't take no more
    Of me and my sparky little cheeky face.

    It would seem at the start
    I would get a good part,
    But now that bubble has burst.
    How can I be
    Something other than me,
    Till we can imagine it first.
    We didn't predict
    I wouldn't get picked
    For romance or a car chase.
    No drama, no glory,
    No sign of a story
    For my chirpy little cheeky face.

RACHAEL goes to get the keyboard.

    Attitudes have moved,
    Things have improved,
    There's a wheelchair on *Gardener's World.*
    It surely must please us
    We're in ads for Maltesers,
    Trumpets sound! Banners unfurled!
    That's what I wanted,
    Things to be fronted
    By crips, isn't that ace?

I thought representation
Would bring such elation
To my cheery little cheeky face.

RACHAEL starts to play the keyboard.

Cheeky face, cheeky face,
There's never been such a cheeky face.
Though life is tough,
It's not the bitter stuff
That we want from your cheeky face.

When I get out of my seat,
'Fucking benefit cheat!'
So are things better for disabled me?
No, it's just a cover
Coz there goes another
Killed by the DWP.
It's the oldest of tricks
'Look! The Paralympics!'
While the deaths gather a-pace,
And as the bodies pile,
It wipes the smile
From my chirpy little cheeky face

Cheeky face, cheeky face,
There's never been such a cheeky face.
Turns out there's still
Those that want to kill
Me and my lovely little cheeky face.

RACHAEL abruptly stops playing the keyboard.

RACHAEL: So audience it may be that we have led you to a
rather bleak place.

LISA: For example, after watching the show one night a lady said…

RACHAEL: 'But what can I do? I'm white and middle class and not disabled…'

LISA: …and she lived in Brighton…

RACHAEL: '…and I live in Brighton – what can I actually do?'

LISA: We said…

RACHAEL: We don't have an answer.

LISA: All we can do is say how it is.

RACHAEL: But having thought about it, there is an answer we wish we'd given her…

LISA: Lovely Brighton Lady, the next time you watch a TV drama or comedy…

RACHAEL: A film, or a play…

LISA: Or even read a book…

RACHAEL: Take a moment. A conscious moment to imagine that the lead character is disabled.

LISA: You don't have to solve any plot issues that might throw up.

RACHAEL: You're not responsible, you don't have to do it all, all you have to do is imagine it.

LISA: Just imagine.

RACHAEL: It won't cause any trouble…

LISA: Because, let's face it, imagining something doesn't change anything.

RACHAEL starts playing an upbeat riff and they sing.

RACHAEL: Some people get up early and go for a run,
    They love to make a green smoothie,
    But you can't do it all,

LISA: When you're four feet tall,

RACHAEL: Or a hard up Mother of three.

LISA: (wouldn't want to)

RACHAEL: Our rhythms go snap, we both love a nap,
    And a bagel and watching TV.
    It costs big time, to always be fine
    But being with you is free.

BOTH: Friendly face, happy face,
    grumpy face, tired face.
    Just like anyone's face,
    Sometimes a cheeky face,
    Or a sparky face is common place.
    We both find it fun
    To say WELL DONE!

RACHAEL: With no mention of your…

LISA: Cheeky,

RACHAEL: Or talk about your…

LISA: Freaky,

RACHAEL: Sometimes you just can't do it all,

LISA: Wouldn't want to do it all,

BOTH: Even if you've got a cheeky face! WOW!

Blackout.

The End.

WWW.OBERONBOOKS.COM

STILL NO IDEA